The Book of *little*
CANADIAN POLITICAL
wisdom

The *little* Book of CANADIAN POLITICAL *wisdom*

Rick Broadhead
& Andy Donato

KEY PORTER BOOKS

Library and Archives Canada Cataloguing in Publication

Broadhead, Rick
    The little book of Canadian political wisdom / Rick Broadhead; illustrated by
Andy Donato.
Includes bibliographical references.
ISBN 1-55263-640-2

    1. Political satire, Canadian (English) 2. Canada—Politics and government—
1993– —Humor. 3. Canadian wit and humor (English)—21st century. I. Donato,
Andy, 1937– II. Title.

PS8375.B76 2004   C817'.608   C2004-903842-7

The publisher gratefully acknowledges the support of the Canada Council for the
Arts and the Ontario Arts Council for its publishing program. We acknowledge the
support of the Government of Ontario through the Ontario Media Development
Corporation's Ontario Book Initiative.

We acknowledge the financial support of the Government of Canada through the
Book Publishing Industry Development Program (BPIDP) for our publishing activities.

Key Porter Books Limited
70 The Esplanade
Toronto, Ontario
Canada M5E 1R2

www.keyporter.com

Cover design: Jack Steiner
Electronic formatting: Jean Lightfoot Peters

Printed and bound in Canada

04 05 06 07 08 5 4 3 2 1

Author's Preface

Canadian politics wouldn't be the same without the verbal barbs, the vigorous shouting matches, the foot-in-the-mouth comments, and the skillful use of wit and humour that characterize political debate and discussion in this country. When I first started working on this collection, I decided I wanted it to be more than just a quote book. In the spirit of *Esquire Magazine's* Dubious Achievement Awards, I wanted to bestow recognition on Canadian politicians for their sharp tongues and wacky comments. Who are the best political mudslingers in Canada? Which politicians have the most acerbic tongues? Who's the master of the political putdown? And which politician is most in need of a refresher course in Canadian geography?

The rules were simple. I had to identify one hundred of the most humorous and outrageous comments ever made by Canadian politicians, past or present, famous or obscure. To find the winners, I combed through thousands of pages of historical and contemporary material—books, debate transcripts, newspaper and magazine archives—looking for quips and comments that made me either laugh or shake my head in disbelief.

A number of notable Canadian politicians—chief among them Jean Chrétien, Tommy Douglas, and John Crosbie—are so legendary for the remarks that have rolled off their tongues, they received multiple honours in this book. Former prime minister Jean Chrétien's hilarious definition of a "proof" is the funniest comment I came across (although his comment about seals in Alberta is a close runner-up). National prominence, however, was not a prerequisite to qualify for an award. Although you'll recognize many of the award recipients, many lesser-known and regional politicians also made my shortlist for being quick (or sloppy) on their feet. One of my favourite off-the-cuff remarks comes from former Alberta MLA Laurence Decore, who referred to one of his esteemed colleagues in the Alberta Legislature as the "Honourable Mousy Minister."

As I begin to work on Volume II of *The Little Book of Canadian Political Wisdom*, I welcome submissions and recollections from readers. What's the best line you've ever heard from a Canadian politician? Whose insults are the most memorable? What's the funniest slip-of-the-tongue you've ever heard? If you'd like to nominate a Canadian politician for a humorous comment or nasty remark, I can be reached at rickb@rickbroadhead.com.

Finally, I'd like to thank Anna Porter and the staff at Key Porter Books for their enthusiastic support of my work; to my talented editor, Janie Yoon, for her invaluable advice and guidance; to Julie Kirsch and her staff at the *Toronto Sun* library for generously sharing their vast (and impressive) research archives with me; to Sherry Johnston and the photo staff at the *Toronto Sun* for their kind assistance; to the amazing Andy Donato for his wonderful illustrations; and to Canadian politicians everywhere without whom this book wouldn't be possible.

Rick Broadhead
September 2004

Illustrator's Preface

While there is no question that politicians have control over what they say (a control that is often disregarded), they have only marginal control over how they look. For political pundits and political cartoonists, misspoken words and even well-turned phrases plant the seed for both commentary and caricaturing. But how they look... well, that's where cartoonists truly zero in, using the magic of satire and the stroke of a pen to make mountains out of molehills. We exaggerate. And that's where the fun lies.

Over the years, Canadian politicians have made it almost too easy. There was Lester Pearson and his bow tie, John Diefenbaker with his jowls, Pierre Trudeau with his almost imperial haughtiness, Joe Clark with his chipmunk-like bumbling, Brian Mulroney with that chin, and Jean Chrétien with his... well, pick one of many. The lopsided grin? The twisted mouth? Da way he talks? So what's a cartoonist like me to do? In the case of Joe Clark, for example, you supply him with mittens attached to a string—all because he once lost his luggage. With Brian Mulroney, that chin becomes the size of an aircraft carrier, and Jean Chrétien (over time, and three successive majority governments) verges on derangement. All in jest, of course.

I have been asked many times how long it takes to do a cartoon. I tell people it takes over thirty years, which is how long I have been in this game, and how long it takes to have the thoughts and insights that guide the pen. Drawing is like brain surgery. Anybody can do it. But not everyone can do it successfully. A cartoonist is like a blind javelin thrower at the Olympics. He's not too accurate, but he sure gets the attention of the spectators.

My thanks to Rick Broadhead for the idea that spawned this book. And to the politicians, of course, who make it so easy.

Andy Donato
September 2004

BEST ACTOR IN A POLITICAL ROLE

"And the award goes to ... "

MOST NONSENSICAL STATEMENT
during a Speech

" Seals don't eat beef. I was interviewed one day in France. I explained one of the problems is we have too many seals. A reporter came to me and asked if it is true that seals eat cod. I don't know. I'm not a seal. But I can tell you seals don't eat beef because the seals are not living in Alberta. "

PRIME MINISTER JEAN CHRÉTIEN
on July 8, 1995, speaking at a Liberal Party
fundraiser in Calgary

BEST AD-HOC SOLUTION
to Our Environmental Problems

" You know, if all of us quit breathing, can you imagine how much carbon dioxide we could avoid sending into the atmosphere? **"**

ALBERTA PREMIER RALPH KLEIN
on February 26, 2002

BEST DESCRIPTION
of Tory Tax Policy

** I have to say that for a Tory to complain about high taxes is like Mike Tyson complaining about somebody biting his ear. **

FEDERAL FINANCE MINISTER PAUL MARTIN,
on April 30, 1999

BEST COMPARISON
of a Prime Minister to a Pop Star

" Paul Martin commits to positions like Britney Spears commits to marriage. **"**

STEPHEN HARPER,
while announcing his candidacy for
the leadership of the Conservative Party of
Canada on January 12, 2004

BEST PROMO SPOT
by a Federal Politician

" Folks, you're watching POT-TV. I'm Jack Layton, Leader of the New Democratic Party of Canada. **"**

FEDERAL NDP LEADER JACK LAYTON
in 2003, during a videotaped interview with POT-TV, a pro-marijuana Web site based in Vancouver

STARTING THE CONSTITUTION WITH 'WE THE PEOPLE' IS SO CLICHÉ, WHY NOT START WITH SOMETHING LIKE 'I, PIERRE ELLIOTT TRUDEAU...'
DONATO
TORONTO SUN

BEST DISPLAY
of Self-esteem

❝ I was my best successor but I decided not to succeed myself. **❞**

FORMER PRIME MINISTER PIERRE TRUDEAU
in November 1984, when asked
what he thought of his successor,
Liberal leader John Turner

MOST CONFUSING PROMISE
by a Politician

" As long as I'm saying what I really think, I'm prepared to stand by it. **"**

KIM CAMPBELL
in an interview with the
Vancouver Sun, 1983

... BUT JEAN, WE WANT DA PROOF OF DA PROOF

BEST IMITATION
of a Mathematician

❝ I don't know, a proof is a proof. What kind of a proof is a proof? A proof is a proof and when you have a good proof it's because it's proven. **❞**

PRIME MINISTER JEAN CHRÉTIEN
on September 5, 2002, trying to explain what type of evidence would prove that Iraq has weapons of mass destruction

BEST SPONTANEOUS INSULT
during a Fit of Rage in the
House of Commons

❝ You little fat little chubby little sucker! **❞**

REFORM MP DARREL STINSON,
referring to federal PC Leader Jean Charest
in the House of Commons on
December 4, 1997

FUNNIEST GEOGRAPHICAL
Gaffe

❝ Just as Lake Erie drains from north to south, there is an ongoing drain in terms of our young people. ❞

CANADIAN ALLIANCE LEADER STOCKWELL DAY on October 24, 2000, during a campaign stop in Niagara Falls, Ontario. (Lake Erie actually runs from south to north, not north to south.)

WORST ADVICE
on the Middle East Conflict

" The best positive thing you can do is not to tell them to stop on both sides to fight and to go back to talk is the only way out of that. And it's what I said and I said that. **"**

PRIME MINISTER JEAN CHRÉTIEN

BEST CHARACTERIZATION
of the Liberal Party

" The Liberals are the flying saucers of politics. No one can make head nor tail of them, and they never are seen twice in the same place. **"**

PRIME MINISTER JOHN DIEFENBAKER,
speaking in London, Ontario, on May 5, 1962

RUNNER-UP: BEST CHARACTERIZATION
of the Liberal Party

" [The Liberals] are a beanbag kind of party that looks like the last person that sat in it. "

BOB RAE
Premier of Ontario, 1990–1995

BEST OBSERVATION
about Canada

" Canada is the greatest nation in this country. "

ALLAN LAMPORT
Mayor of Toronto, 1952–1954

BEST QUIP
about Canada–U.S. Trade

" Our essential exports to you are hockey players and cold fronts. Our main imports from you are baseball players and acid rain. **"**

PRIME MINISTER PIERRE TRUDEAU

on July 13, 1982, speaking to a large U.S. audience in Montreal at the annual baseball commissioner's luncheon

BEST DEFENCE
to Allegations of Conduct
Unbecoming a Politician

❝ My conduct had nothing to do with me. **❞**

FORMER ONTARIO MPP AND SPEAKER OF THE ONTARIO LEGISLATURE AL MCLEAN, defending his conduct during a sexual harassment case, in an interview with the *Orillia Packet and Times* in July 2000

WORST VERBAL GAFFE
during a Federal Election

" [An election] is not the time, I don't think, to get involved in very, very serious discussions. "

PRIME MINISTER KIM CAMPBELL

on September 23, 1993, during a campaign stop in St. Bruno, Quebec

44

BEST DISPLAY OF SELF-CONFIDENCE
by a Politician

" I never laid an egg either, but I know more about making an omelette than a hen does. **"**

T.C. (TOMMY) DOUGLAS,

replying to federal Agriculture Minister James Gardiner, who asked him, "What do you know about farming?—you're not a farmer."

WORST DISPLAY OF SELF-CONFIDENCE
by a Politician

" I know as much about housing as you can put on the head of a pin and still have room left over for the Lord's Prayer. **"**

ONTARIO MUNICIPAL AFFAIRS AND HOUSING MINISTER AL LEACH

in a speech on August 21, 1995

MOST HUMOROUS GAFFE
during a White House Press Conference

Reporter: Sir, this is a question for both of you. The records show that there are far more drugs coming over the border from Canada into the United States now than ever before. Can you look into that and maybe do something about it—both of you?
Jean Chrétien: It's more trade.

This exchange took place at the White House on April 8, 1997, during a press conference hosted by U.S. President Bill Clinton and Prime Minister Jean Chrétien. After Clinton clarified the reporter's question, Chrétien said he thought the reporter had asked about "trucks" not "drugs."

BEST REMARK
about Regionalism

" Canada is like an old cow. The West feeds it. Ontario and Quebec milk it. And you can well imagine what it's doing in the Maritimes. **"**

**FORMER SASKATCHEWAN PREMIER
T.C. (TOMMY) DOUGLAS,**
speaking in Weyburn, Saskatchewan,
on June 29, 1983

MOST BONEHEADED REMARK
by a Liberal Leader

" I'm not going to play politics on the floor of the House of Commons. **"**

LIBERAL LEADER JOHN TURNER
on October 1, 1987, speaking in the
House of Commons

BEST BOXING METAPHOR
during a Leadership Race

" How boring is he? It's said that if he were going down for the third time, someone else's life would flash before his eyes. "

DESCRIPTION OF DENNIS TIMBRELL,
a candidate for the leadership of the Ontario Progressive Conservative Party, that was circulating in the 1980s

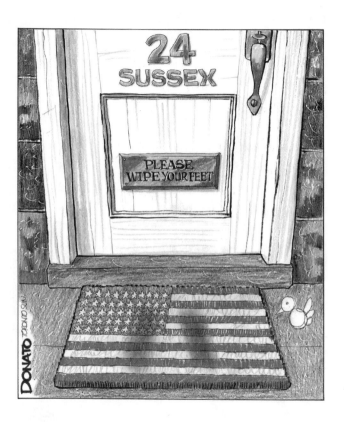

BEST EXCUSE
for Blaming the Americans

> If you're a mayor and you have a problem, what do you do? You blame the provincial government. And when you're the provincial government and you have a problem, what do you do? You blame the federal government. And for us, we cannot blame the Queen any more, so we blame the Americans once in a while.

PRIME MINISTER JEAN CHRÉTIEN,
in an interview with Peter Gzowski on
CBC Radio, March 1, 1995

MOST UNUSUAL ADVICE
from a Politician

" Popularity is bad for you...I try to avoid it like the plague, and I've been reasonably successful. **"**

PRIME MINISTER BRIAN MULRONEY
in May 1992, as he campaigned for his
third majority government

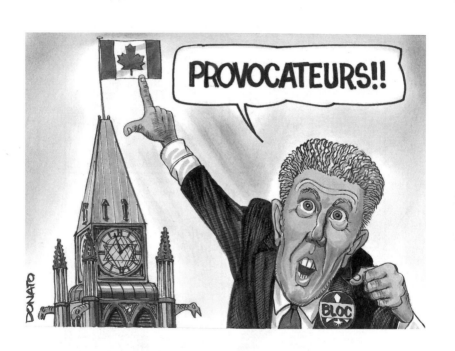

BEST LINE
from a Quebec Separatist

❝ It takes a sovereignist for two federalists to talk to each other. **❞**

BLOC QUÉBÉCOIS LEADER GILLES DUCEPPE
in 2004

BEST CHARACTERIZATION
of Political Life in Canada

" You don't need brains for this job, just physical stamina. **"**

NEW DEMOCRAT MP AUDREY MCLAUGHLIN
on December 2, 1989, a few hours before
winning the NDP leadership

MOST LUDICROUS EXPLANATION
for a Military Plane Crash

" It is part of the ups and downs of any war plane. "

FEDERAL DEFENSE MINISTER GILLES LAMONTAGNE
in the House of Commons on May 24, 1983

BEST DISPLAY
of New Brunswick Pride

" Once you've been premier of New Brunswick, why would you want to become prime minister of Canada? **"**

NEW BRUNSWICK PREMIER FRANK MCKENNA
in an interview with the *Halifax Daily News*
in October 1997

WORST DISPLAY
of New Brunswick Pride

" I was elected to run New Brunswick. No one said I had to live there. **"**

NEW BRUNSWICK PREMIER RICHARD HATFIELD,
defending his regular jaunts outside
the province

BEST DEFINITION
of Economic Prosperity

" A recession is when your neighbour loses his job. A depression is when you lose your own job. Economic recovery is when Pierre Trudeau loses his job. "

FUTURE CONSERVATIVE LEADER BRIAN MULRONEY
in May 1982, speaking at a Toronto fundraiser

BEST APPROACH
to Crime Prevention

" We want our police force equipped with the best, the most expensive equipment, the finest bullets. **"**

ALLAN LAMPORT
Mayor of Toronto, 1952–1954

STRANGEST INSULT
by a Premier

" [Mr. McGuinty] just says whatever pops into his little, sharp, pointy head because he thinks that's what you want to hear. "

ONTARIO PREMIER ERNIE EVES
on September 30, 2003, referring to Ontario
Liberal Leader Dalton McGuinty

BEST COMEBACK
from an Insult

What if I spear you with my head?

ONTARIO LIBERAL LEADER DALTON MCGUINTY,
joking with the hosts of a Toronto radio show
on October 1, 2003, the day after Premier
Ernie Eves said McGuinty had a
"sharp, pointy head"

AH... THE CLARITY OF DEBATE

MOST CONFUSING QUESTION POSED
in the House of Commons

" When will the Liberals stop adopting the policy that they will give to those who should get, on the basis that those who have got have to give back that which they got in order to get that which they got, such that what they got was for nought? **"**

ALBERTA CONSERVATIVE MP ARNOLD MALONE
in the House of Commons on March 16, 1983

WORST ARGUMENT FOR FEWER WOMEN
in the House of Commons

" Forgive me for saying this, but what would happen if we were all PMSed the same week? Can you imagine what the Parliament of Canada would be like? **"**

REFORM MP DEBORAH GREY
on March 20, 1997, speaking about the dangers of having too many women in the House of Commons

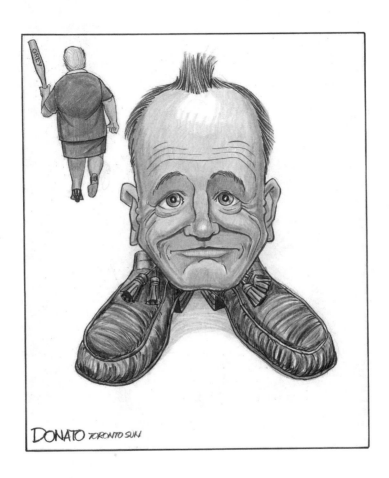

DONATO *TORONTO SUN*

MOST CONFUSING
Communications Plan

❝ My strategy has always been to stay on course unless a change, of course, is announced. And if it is, of course, we will announce it. **❞**

PRIME MINISTER JOHN TURNER
on July 4, 1984, speaking about his government's economic policies

BEST POLITICAL
Riddle

❝ What's the difference between a catfish and a politician? One is a wide-mouthed, bottom-feeding scum sucker. The other is a fish. **❞**

REFORM PARTY LEADER PRESTON MANNING,
speaking to audiences in Ontario
in January 1992

" What is the difference between a cactus and a conservative caucus? On a cactus, the pricks are all on the outside. "

JOHN DIEFENBAKER,
Prime Minister of Canada,
1957–1963

MOST UNFLATTERING REMARK
about Jean Chrétien

“ My feeling for this prime minister is such that if God asked me to go to heaven with him, I'd have to thank God but turn him down. **”**

PROGRESSIVE CONSERVATIVE SENATOR CONSIGLIO DI NINO
in 1998

MOST AMBITIOUS PROMISE
by a Member of Parliament

" If my constituents wanted me to sit as an independent from Mars, I would do it. **"**

REFORM MP IAN MCCLELLAND
on April 16, 1998, in an interview with
the *Globe and Mail*

STILL WAITING

BEST GRASP
of the Obvious

" As long as I am Prime Minister, I remain the Prime Minister. **"**

PRIME MINISTER JEAN CHRÉTIEN
on January 15, 2002, brushing off any
suggestions that he might be retiring

BEST PUT-DOWN
of the Canadian Army

❝ If it's a war between the [Canadian] armed
services and the Indians, I'll take the
Indians. **❞**

FORMER SASKATCHEWAN ATTORNEY GENERAL
ROY ROMANOW
in March 1983

BEST THREAT
by a Prime Minister

" I took him out, and I can take you out too. **"**

PRIME MINISTER JEAN CHRÉTIEN
in 1996, speaking to the media after being accosted by a protester in Ottawa

MOST EMBARRASSING APPEARANCE
on CNN

" They don't know what they're talking about. I don't know who this group is. I've never heard of them before. I had never seen them before... They're located somewhere in Geneva. **"**

TORONTO MAYOR MEL LASTMAN
on April 24, 2003, in the midst of Toronto's SARS crisis, telling CNN anchor Aaron Brown that he has never heard of the World Health Organization

BEST TONGUE-IN-CHEEK ENDORSEMENT
of a Sitting Prime Minister

" All I can say to the Prime Minister is that he is my favourite candidate, and I am pulling for him to be the next Leader of the Opposition. "

LIBERAL LEADER JOHN TURNER,
referring to Prime Minister Brian Mulroney in
the House of Commons, October 3, 1986

BEST MOTIVATION
for Becoming a Politician

❝ The reason you get into politics is because you don't want to be governed by people less good than yourself. **❞**

PRIME MINISTER PIERRE TRUDEAU
on December 14, 1978

MOST EMBARRASSING REMARK
on an Airplane

❝ Let's face it, there's no whore like an old whore. If I'd been in Bryce's position, I'd have been right in there with my nose in the public trough like the rest of them...I hope this is all off the record. ❞

FEDERAL CONSERVATIVE LEADER BRIAN MULRONEY
on July 14, 1984, speaking about Liberal MP Bryce Mackasey's patronage appointment as ambassador to Portugal

BEST MANGLED METAPHOR
by a Politician

" If this thing starts to snowball, it will catch fire right across the country. **"**

ROBERT THOMPSON,
Leader of the Social Credit Party
of Canada, 1961–1967

RUNNER-UP: BEST MANGLED METAPHOR
by a Politician

" The leopard, Mr. Speaker, cannot change its stripes! **"**

BRITISH COLUMBIA MLA DON PHILLIPS,
speaking in the British Columbia
Legislature and warning us that some
people just don't change

BEST ATTEMPT TO BREAK
the Ice during a Heated Dispute
with the Americans

"

Gentlemen, we all must realize that neither side has any monopoly on sons of bitches. "

LIBERAL CABINET MINISTER C.D. HOWE,
representing Canada at a Washington DC
meeting to resolve a shipping dispute

MOST CREATIVE USE
of Song Lyrics

❝ Sheila Copps is running in a certain race for the leadership of the Liberal party. It reminds me of an old song. It goes: 'Pass me the tequila, Sheila, and lie down and love me again.' **❞**

INTERNATIONAL TRADE MINISTER JOHN CROSBIE,
speaking at a Tory fundraiser in Victoria,
British Columbia, on February 27, 1990

BEST EXAMPLE
of Political Backpedalling

** The fact is the statements are perfectly consistent—but more importantly, I don't have all the facts. **

PRIME MINISTER PAUL MARTIN
on April 7, 2004, defending his seemingly
contradictory statements on financial
mismanagement within the
federal government

WITTIEST REMARK
by a Federal Transportation Minister

" No one can understand airline fares. Why I should be expected to understand them is beyond me. **"**

FEDERAL TRANSPORTATION MINISTER JOHN CROSBIE
on February 24, 1988

BEST EXPLANATION
for a Physical Disability

" It's true, I speak out of one side of my mouth. I'm not a Tory. I don't speak out of both sides of my mouth. **"**

PRIME MINISTER JEAN CHRÉTIEN
on September 27, 1993, poking fun at his speech impediment, which was caused by a childhood illness

MOST CONTROVERSIAL
Ornithological Reference in the House of Commons

ff Just quieten down, baby . . . the titmice can quieten down. **JJ**

FEDERAL JUSTICE MINISTER JOHN CROSBIE,
calling Sheila Copps a "titmouse"
(a type of bird) in the House of Commons,
June 4, 1985

BEST INSULT
by a Saskatchewan Politician

My honourable friend on the other side of the House is big enough to swallow me, and if he did he would have more brains in his belly than he has in his head.

SASKATCHEWAN PREMIER T.C. (TOMMY) DOUGLAS,
speaking to Walter Tucker, the
Liberal Leader of Saskatchewan, in the
Saskatchewan Legislature

❝ And how much does Mr. Tucker weigh? About 230 pounds, it is true. Even at that, it's a high price to pay for baloney. **❞**

SASKATCHEWAN PREMIER T.C. (TOMMY) DOUGLAS,
referring to Walter Tucker, the
Liberal Leader of Saskatchewan

BIGGEST FOOT-IN-THE-MOUTH COMMENT
by a Member of Parliament

" Damn Americans, I hate those bastards. **"**

LIBERAL MP CAROLYN PARRISH
outside the House of Commons on
February 26, 2003, expressing her disgust
at U.S. plans to attack Iraq

BIGGEST FOOT-IN-THE-MOUTH COMMENT
by a Mayor

" What the hell do I want to go to a place like Mombasa [Kenya]? Snakes just scare the hell out of me. I'm sort of scared about going there, but the wife is really nervous. I just see myself in a pot of boiling water with all these natives dancing around me. **"**

TORONTO MAYOR MEL LASTMAN
in June 2001, prior to departing for Kenya to promote Toronto's 2008 Olympic bid

MOST APOLOGIES
by a Politician

"I am truly sorry, and I'm going to say it again, I'm sorry my comments were inappropriate. And I want to apologize to everyone for my remarks, particularly anyone who was offended by them...I am sorry I made the remarks...I am sorry I made the remarks...I'm sorry I made the remarks...I am truly sorry...I am truly sorry I made those remarks...I am truly sorry..."

TORONTO MAYOR MEL LASTMAN,
apologizing for his offensive remarks about Africa during Toronto's 2008 Olympic bid. Lastman apologized no fewer than twenty times at a press conference on June 21, 2001.

BEST MOCKERY
of Liberal Economic Policy

❝ All the evidence suggests that the Liberals want to look after impoverished Canadians— why else would they have created over four million of them? **❞**

FEDERAL PC LEADER BRIAN MULRONEY
in 1984

123

MOST GULLIBLE
Politician

❝ Mr. Speaker, there are two visitors in the House today. Miss Conny Lingus from Cherryvale and Mr. Jack Meoff from Falkland. Please make them feel welcome. **❞**

BRITISH COLUMBIA MLA PATRICIA JORDAN,
after being fooled by reporters on
April Fool's Day, 1976

BEST ARGUMENT
to Be the Prime Minister of Canada

" Most Canadians know that when you want to get finances in order, you confide them to a woman. **"**

DEFENSE MINISTER KIM CAMPBELL,
speaking at a federal PC leadership debate in Montreal, April 21, 1993

MOST OFFENSIVE REMARK
That Was Not Ruled Offensive

❝ He is nothing but a blowhard windbag who in my opinion is a waste of skin. **❞**

REFORM MP ALLAN KERPAN,
referring to Liberal MP Steve Mahoney in the
House of Commons on April 15, 1999

BEST SELF-DEPRECATING
Joke by a Politician

“ I've been called treacherous, stupid, venal, lazy ... and that's only by the Tories. **”**

FEDERAL PC LEADER PETER MCKAY,
speaking at the annual Parliamentary Press Gallery Dinner in June 2003

RUNNER-UP: BEST SELF-DEPRECATING
Joke by a Politician

" They say I'm so longwinded it takes me fifteen minutes to clear my throat. **"**

ONTARIO PREMIER WILLIAM DAVIS
in 1985

132

BEST METAPHORICAL ATTACK
on a Conservative Party Leader

" Brian Mulroney is the 'head reptile among a party of political chameleons.' "

LIBERAL MP JOHN EVANS,
colourfully criticizing federal PC Leader
Brian Mulroney in the House of Commons
on February 10, 1984

MOST INCOHERENT SENTENCE
during a Radio Interview

" My style of leadership, uh, and in my former role as well, was to state what my idea was but also to encourage, uh, you know, I know what I know and I know what I don't know. **"**

CONSERVATIVE PARTY LEADERSHIP CANDIDATE BELINDA STRONACH,
being interviewed on a Winnipeg radio station on January 21, 2004

STRANGEST CASE
of Temporary Colour Blindness

❝ It's great to be in Stoney Creek with Brad and our four Liberal, er, our four Conservative candidates... ❞

ONTARIO CONSERVATIVE PREMIER ERNIE EVES, speaking in Stoney Creek, Ontario, on September 30, 2003, just days before a provincial election. (Eves later conceded that he "got his colour schemes mixed up.")

BEST JOKE
about a Prime Minister's Speech

" Someone has given me a copy of the Prime Minister's speech. I don't know why they bothered. There's nothing in it. **"**

FEDERAL PROGRESSIVE CONSERVATIVE PARTY LEADER JOHN DIEFENBAKER,

campaigning in Stratford, Ontario, in 1957

MOST EMBARRASSING
Historical Goof by a Federal Politician

" …Dieppe, like Vichy more than two decades earlier, attests to our pride as a nation in defence of freedom and justice. **"**

FEDERAL DEFENSE MINISTER JOHN MCCALLUM,
in a letter to the editor of the *National Post* on August 31, 2002. (McCallum meant to say "Vimy," not "Vichy." Vichy was the capital city established by the Nazis during their occupation of France.)

RUNNER-UP: MOST EMBARRASSING
Historical Goof by a Federal Politician

" Sixty years ago, Canadians were working alongside their British and American allies planning for the invasion of Norway and the liberation of Europe... Today, it is every bit as important that Canada step forward—just as we did during the invasion of Norway. **"**

PRIME MINISTER PAUL MARTIN,
speaking to troops at CFB Gagetown in New Brunswick in April 2004. (Canada invaded Normandy, not Norway.)

WITTIEST ANALOGY
during a Federal Election Campaign

"Any politician who thinks you can stimulate a $700-billion GNP economy with some sewer projects or $2 or $3 billion in public works, he will believe you can start a 747 with a flashlight battery."

REFORM PARTY LEADER PRESTON MANNING
on September 10, 1993, ridiculing Liberal
Leader Jean Chrétien's economic plan

LEAST ELOQUENT INSULT
in a Provincial Legislature

" You, sir, are one of the crappiest speakers I've ever seen. **"**

ALBERTA MLA NICK TAYLOR,
speaking to David Carter, Speaker of the
Alberta Legislature, on May 13, 1991

MOST EMBARRASSING
Unintentional Insult

66 I'm not against abused women. I'm in favour of them 100 per cent. 99

NIAGARA FALLS REGIONAL CITY COUNCILLOR
DOUG MANN

in 1990, trying to argue against increased
funding for women's shelters

RUNNER-UP: MOST EMBARRASSING
Unintentional Insult

" Your majesty, I thank you from the bottom of my heart, and Madame Houde here thanks you from her bottom, too. "

MONTREAL MAYOR CAMILLIEN HOUDE
in 1939, speaking to King George VI
during his Canadian tour

BEST MORALE BOOST
for Municipal Politicians

" There are several things I envy about municipal politicians. One is that most of you have a fixed term in office. Some of you have found two years to be too short. It's better than seven months. **"**

FEDERAL PC LEADER JOE CLARK
on June 10, 1982, poking fun at his very short term as Prime Minister of Canada

MOST VULGAR REACTION
upon Becoming Prime Minister
of Canada

" I've inherited an unbelievable bag of shit! **"**

PRIME MINISTER JOHN TURNER
in 1984, speaking to his campaign manager
about the terrible mess (including a large
deficit) he inherited from his predecessor,
Pierre Elliott Trudeau

BEST QUIP
about the State of Canada's Military

What I'm worried about is the lack of military build-up that we've got in Canada...Down in Newfoundland, we can hardly sleep for wondering when St. Pierre and Miquelon are going to invade.

NEWFOUNDLAND MP JOHN CROSBIE

on March 21, 1983, speaking at a press conference while campaigning for the leadership of the federal Progressive Conservative Party

BEST REMARK
by a Member of Parliament after Invoking a Point of Order in the House of Commons

" I rise on a point of order. Is the relevancy rule to be applied or will this jackass be allowed to continue? "

PROGRESSIVE CONSERVATIVE MP DAVID KILGOUR,
referring to Liberal MP Jean-Jacques Blais in
the House of Commons on May 4, 1982

MOST BIZARRE POLITICAL INSULT
during a Provincial Election Campaign

" Dalton McGuinty. He's an evil reptilian kitten-eater from another planet. **"**

DESCRIPTION OF ONTARIO LIBERAL LEADER DALTON MCGUINTY

contained in a news release issued
by the Ontario Progressive Conservatives
on September 12, 2003

BEST REFERENCE
to a Cabinet Minister's Cold

" I am sorry the Minister is suffering from a cold, but even if she had been in better voice and better health, she would have undoubtedly choked on that budget before she finished her speech. "

LIBERAL LEADER JOHN TURNER
in the House of Commons on March 5, 1986,
speaking to Barbara McDougall, the
Conservative Minister of State for Finance

160

CRUELLEST COMMENT
about Newfoundland

❝ I sometimes felt we would be better off if we towed it out to sea and sank it. **❞**

DONALD BLENKARN, ONTARIO TORY MP AND CHAIRMAN OF THE HOUSE OF COMMONS FINANCE COMMITTEE,
speaking on June 21, 1990,
in Kitchener, Ontario

BEST INSULT
in the Alberta Legislature

" Mr. Speaker, the minister acts like a mouse, squeaks like a mouse, and is a mouse...My last question is to the Honourable Mousy Minister. "

ALBERTA MLA LAURENCE DECORE
on June 21, 1991

RUNNER-UP: BEST INSULT
in the Alberta Legislature

" Why don't you get an operation and have your lips attached to your brain? **"**

ALBERTA JUSTICE MINISTER JON HAVELOCK,
speaking to Liberal MLA Linda Sloan on
May 12, 1997

164

BEST QUIP
to a Horde of Trailing Journalists

" Watch out for the wall—as much as I'd like to see some of you guys hit it. **"**

STEPHEN HARPER,
during the Conservative Party Leadership
Convention in Toronto, March 2004

MOST EMBARRASSING OPEN-MIKE
Gaffe by a Prime Minister

❝ I like to stand up to the Americans. It's popular...people like it, but you have to be very careful because they're our friends. **❞**

PRIME MINISTER JEAN CHRÉTIEN
at a NATO summit on July 9, 1997, during what he thought was a private conservation with the Belgian Prime Minister

HARSHEST VERBAL ATTACK
by a Canadian Mayor

" He's the greatest argument for birth control that I've ever come across. "

TORONTO MAYOR MEL LASTMAN,
speaking to reporters on April 1, 1998, referring to Toronto City Councillor Michael Walker

BEST ANSWER TO THE QUESTION
"Who Are You and Where Are You Going?"

❝ I live here, and I'm going to the bathroom. **❞**

PRIME MINISTER LESTER PEARSON

in 1967, speaking to a U.S. Secret Service agent who confronted him inside his house at Harrington Lake, the official prime ministerial cottage in the Gatineau Hills. Secret Service agents were there to protect U.S. President Lyndon Johnson, who was in Canada for Expo 67 and a brief meeting with Pearson.

BEST DENIAL
by a Prime Minister

" I am not denying anything I did not say. "

PRIME MINISTER BRIAN MULRONEY

in September 1986, attempting to clarify his
position on mandatory drug testing

MOST CONFUSING DESCRIPTION
of a Federal Budget

" The budget is stimulative. It is less stimulative than if it had been more, but it is more than if it had been less. **"**

PRIME MINISTER PIERRE TRUDEAU,
speaking to reporters in May 1982

BEST USE OF
Canadian Geography to Insult a Tory

" He is one of the most inflexible, obstinate Tories I have ever encountered. He's like Pre-Cambrian Shield in human form. **"**

ONTARIO NDP LEADER STEPHEN LEWIS,
referring to Ontario Conservative MPP
Don Irvine in the 1970s

WORST GREETING
to a Serbian Audience

“ Good afternoon, Croatian people. **”**

SHEILA COPPS,

while campaigning for office in the Ontario
provincial election of 1977. Copps lost by
fourteen votes.

THE NEW IMAGE

179

BEST EUPHEMISM
for "Shut Up"

" There is an old saying that it is very difficult to hear when your mouth is open. **"**

SPEAKER MYRNA PHILLIPS
of the Manitoba Legislature, trying to silence
Conservative MLA Don Orchard in July 1986

RUNNER-UP: BEST EUPHEMISM
for "Shut Up"

" Go sit on your mouth. **"**

ALLAN LAMPORT,
speaking to Toronto Council Member John
Sewell. Lamport was Mayor of Toronto
between 1952 and 1954

BEST OBSERVATION
about the Parliament of Canada

" To the young members [of Parliament] who have just come in, I would say that for the first six months after you are here you will wonder how you got here. Then after that, you will wonder how the rest of the members ever got here. "

FORMER PRIME MINISTER JOHN DIEFENBAKER,
speaking in the House of Commons on
September 18, 1968

MOST CONTROVERSIAL JOKE
about Sexual Harassment

" Apparently, just about everybody who quits their job is being sexually harassed. We must have one hell of a lot of attractive people working. If this is the case, I have to admit to you that I have never been sexually harassed...If I were, I would certainly want to make it known that I had been so favoured. **"**

FEDERAL FISHERIES MINISTER JOHN CROSBIE on February 11, 1993. Crosbie was speaking about proposed changes to the unemployment insurance system that would give benefits to workers who could prove sexual harassment.

BEST PUT-DOWN
of One's Own Political Party

" Trying to get a commitment from our own government is like trying to walk across an ocean full of whipped cream on snowshoes. "

TORY MP BOB HICKS

in the House of Commons on December 3, 1986, expressing frustration with his government for delaying a vote on capital punishment

BEST REACTION TO REALIZING
You're Going to Be the Next Prime Minister of Canada

“ Okay, we've won. What do we do now? **”**

BRIAN MULRONEY,
after winning a landslide victory
in the 1984 federal election

PRIMARY SOURCES

Most Nonsensical Statement during a Speech: *Ottawa Citizen*, July 9, 1995.

Best Ad-hoc Solution to Our Environmental Problems: *Globe and Mail*, February 27, 2002.

Best Description of Tory Tax Policy: *Globe and Mail*, May 1, 1999.

Best Comparison of a Prime Minister to a Pop Star: Canadian Press, January 12, 2004.

Best Promo Spot by a Federal Politician: POT-TV Web site (www.pot-tv.net).

Best Display of Self-Esteem: *Globe and Mail*, November 21, 1984.

Most Confusing Promise by a Politician: *Vancouver Sun*, August 29, 1985.

Best Imitation of a Mathematician: *CBC News*, September 5, 2002.

Best Spontaneous Insult during a Fit of Rage in the House of Commons: *Globe and Mail*, December 5, 1997.

Funniest Geographical Gaffe: *Globe and Mail*, October 25, 2000.

Worst Advice on the Middle East Conflict: *Saturday Night*, May 2002.

Best Characterization of the Liberal Party: *I Never Say Anything Provocative: Witticisms, Anecdotes and Reflections by Canada's Most Outspoken Politician*, compiled by Margaret Wente (P. Martin Associates, 1975).

Runner-Up: Best Characterization of the Liberal Party: *Toronto Star*, August 5, 1999.

Best Observation about Canada: *Metro's Goldwyn Mayor: The Complete Malapropisms of Allan Lamport* by John Robert Colombo (Colombo and Company, 1995).

Best Quip about Canada–U.S. Trade: *Globe and Mail*, July 14, 1982.

Best Defence to Allegations of Conduct Unbecoming a Politician: *Orillia Packet & Times*, July 15, 2000.

Worst Verbal Gaffe during a Federal Election: *Toronto Star*, September 24, 1993.

Best Display of Self-Confidence by a Politician: *Douglas in Saskatchewan* by Robert Tyre (Mitchell Press, 1962).

Worst Display of Self-Confidence by a Politician: *Globe and Mail*, August 22, 1995.

Most Humorous Gaffe during a White House Press Conference: *Weekly Compilation of Presidential Documents*, April 14, 1997.

Best Remark about Regionalism: *Globe and Mail*, June 30, 1983.

Most Boneheaded Remark by a Liberal Leader: *Ottawa Citizen*, October 1, 1987.

Best Boxing Metaphor during a Leadership Race: *Canadian Political Babble* by David Olive (John Wiley & Sons, 1993).

Best Excuse for Blaming the Americans: *Globe and Mail*, March 2, 1995.

Most Unusual Advice from a Politician: *Reuters*, May 8, 1992.

Best Line from a Quebec Separatist: *Montreal Gazette*, May 14, 2004.

Best Characterization of Political Life in Canada: *Toronto Star*, December 3, 1989.

Most Ludicrous Explanation for a Military Plane Crash: *Globe and Mail*, May 25, 1983; House of Commons Debates, May 24, 1983.

Best Display of New Brunswick Pride: *Halifax Daily News*, October 9, 1997.

Worst Display of New Brunswick Pride: *Malice in Blunderland, or, How the Grits Stole Christmas* by Allan Fotheringham (Key Porter Books, 1982).

Best Definition of Economic Prosperity: *Globe and Mail*, May 7, 1982.

Best Approach to Crime Prevention: *Metro's Goldwyn Mayor: The*

Complete Malapropisms of Allan Lamport by John Robert Colombo (Colombo and Company, 1995).

Strangest Insult by a Premier: Canadian Press, September 30, 2003.

Best Comeback from an Insult: Canadian Press, October 1, 2003.

Most Confusing Question Posed in the House of Commons: *Globe and Mail*, March 19, 1983; House of Commons Debates, March 16, 1983.

Worst Argument for Fewer Women in the House of Commons: *Globe and Mail*, March 22, 1997.

Most Confusing Communications Plan: *Globe and Mail*, July 5, 1984.

Best Political Riddle: *Toronto Star*, January 26, 1992.

Runner-Up: Best Political Riddle: *The Oxford Book of Canadian Political Anecdotes*, edited by Jack McLeod (Oxford University Press, 1988).

Most Unflattering Remark about Jean Chrétien: *Globe and Mail*, May 6, 1998.

Most Ambitious Promise by a Member of Parliament: *Globe and Mail*, April 17, 1998.

Best Grasp of the Obvious: Canadian Press, January 15, 2002.

Best Put-down of the Canadian Army: *Globe and Mail*, March 19, 1983.

Best Threat by a Prime Minister: *Globe and Mail*, August 22, 2002.

Most Embarrassing Appearance on CNN: *Globe and Mail*, April 26 2003.

Best Tongue-in-Cheek Endorsement of a Sitting Prime Minister: *The Leaders Speak*, compiled by Pamela Chichinskas and Lynette Stokes (Penguin Books Canada, 1988).

Best Motivation for Becoming a Politician: *Globe and Mail*, December 15, 1978.

Most Embarrassing Remark on an Airplane: *Globe and Mail*, July 17, 1984.

Best Mangled Metaphor by a Politician: *Toronto Star*, December 26, 1974.

Runner-Up: Best Mangled Metaphor by a Politician: *Victoria Times-Colonist*, January 31, 1999.

Best Attempt to Break the Ice during a Heated Dispute with the Americans: *Toronto Star*, December 17, 1988.

Most Creative Use of Song Lyrics: *Toronto Star*, March 2, 1990.

Best Example of Political Backpedalling: Canadian Press, April 7, 2004.

Wittiest Remark by a Federal Transportation Minister: *Toronto Star*, February 25, 1988.

Best Explanation for a Physical Disability: *Toronto Star*, September 28, 1993.

Most Controversial Ornithological Reference in the House of Commons: *Montreal Gazette*, June 5, 1985; House of Commons Debates, June 4, 1985.

Best Insult by a Saskatchewan Politician: *Douglas in Saskatchewan* by Robert Tyre (Mitchell Press, 1962).

Runner-Up: Best Insult by a Saskatchewan Politician: *Douglas in Saskatchewan* by Robert Tyre (Mitchell Press, 1962).

Biggest Foot-in-the-Mouth Comment by a Member of Parliament: Canadian Press, February 27, 2003.

Biggest Foot-in-the-Mouth Comment by a Mayor: Reuters, June 22, 2001.

Most Apologies by a Politician: *Globe and Mail*, June 22, 2001.

Best Mockery of Liberal Economic Policy: *The Leaders Speak*, compiled by Pamela Chichinskas and Lynette Stokes (Penguin Books Canada, 1988).

Most Gullible Politician: *Slightly Higher in Canada: A Treasury of Canadian Lore* by John Robert Colombo (Colombo and Company, 1996).

Best Argument to Be the Prime Minister of Canada: *Globe and Mail*, April 22, 1993.

Most Offensive Remark That Was Not Ruled Offensive: *National Post*, April 17, 1999; *Hansard*, April 15, 1990.

Best Self-Deprecating Joke by a Politician: CBC News Viewpoint (www.cbc.ca/news/viewpoint) by Larry Zolf, June 17, 2003.

Runner-Up: Best Self-Deprecating Joke by a Politician: *Canadian Political Babble* by David Olive (John Wiley and Sons, 1993).

Best Metaphorical Attack on a Conservative Party Leader: *Globe and Mail*, February 11, 1984.

Most Incoherent Sentence during a Radio Interview: *Edmonton Journal*, January 25, 2004.

Strangest Case of Temporary Colour Blindness: Canadian Press, September 30, 2003.

Best Joke about a Prime Minister's Speech: *Diefenbaker: Remembering the Chief* by Thad McIlroy (Doubleday Canada, 1984).

Most Embarrassing Historical Goof by a Federal Politician: *National Post*, August 31, 2002; September 3, 2002.

Runner-Up: Most Embarrassing Historical Goof by a Federal Politician: Canadian Press, April 15, 2004.

Wittiest Analogy during a Federal Election Campaign: *Toronto Star*, September 11, 1993.

Least Eloquent Insult in a Provincial Legislature: Alberta Hansard, May 13, 1991.

Most Embarrassing Unintentional Insult: *St. Catharines Standard*, September 6, 1990.

Runner-Up: Most Embarrassing Unintentional Insult: *Ottawa Citizen*, February 20, 2002.

Best Morale Boost for Municipal Politicians: *Globe and Mail*, January 1, 1983.

Most Vulgar Reaction upon Becoming Prime Minister of Canada: *Reign of Error: The Inside Story of John Turner's Troubled Leadership* by Greg Weston (McGraw-Hill Ryerson, 1988).

Best Quip about the State of Canada's Military: *Globe and Mail*, March 22, 1983.

Best Remark by a Member of Parliament after Invoking a Point of Order in the House of Commons: *Globe and Mail*, May 7, 1982.

Most Bizarre Political Insult during a Provincial Election Campaign: *Globe and Mail*, September 13, 2003.

Best Reference to a Cabinet Minister's Cold: *The Leaders Speak*, compiled by Pamela Chichinskas and Lynette Stokes (Penguin Books Canada, 1988).

Cruellest Comment about Newfoundland: *Toronto Star*, June 23, 1990.

Best Insult in the Alberta Legislature: *Calgary Herald*, February 21, 1999; Alberta Hansard, June 21, 1991.

Runner-Up: Best Insult in the Alberta Legislature: *Calgary Herald*, May 13, 1997; Alberta Hansard, May 12, 1997.

Best Quip to a Horde of Trailing Journalists: *Globe and Mail*, March 22, 2004.

Most Embarrassing Open-Mike Gaffe by a Prime Minister: *Toronto Star*, July 10, 1997.

Harshest Verbal Attack by a Canadian Mayor: *Toronto Star*, April 2, 1998.

Best Answer to the Question "Who Are You and Where Are You Going?": *Mike: The Memoirs of the Rt. Hon. Lester B. Pearson*, Volume 3, edited by John A. Monro and Alex I. Inglis (University of Toronto Press, 1975).

Best Denial by a Prime Minister: *Globe and Mail*, September 18, 1986.

Most Confusing Description of a Federal Budget: *Globe and Mail*, May 20, 1982.

Best Use of Canadian Geography to Insult a Tory: *Montreal Gazette*, June 3, 2000.

Worst Greeting to a Serbian Audience: *Nobody's Baby: A Survival Guide to Politics* by Sheila Copps (Deneau, 1996).

Best Euphemism for "Shut Up": *Montreal Gazette*, July 14, 1986.

Runner-Up: Best Euphemism for "Shut Up": *Metro's Goldwyn Mayor: The Complete Malapropisms of Allan Lamport* by John Robert Colombo (Colombo and Company, 1995).

Best Observation about the Parliament of Canada: *I Never Say Anything Provocative: Witticisms, Anecdotes and Reflections by Canada's Most Outspoken Politician*, compiled by Margaret Wente (P. Martin Associates, 1975).

Most Controversial Joke about Sexual Harassment: *Globe and Mail*, February 13, 1993.

Best Put-down of One's Own Political Party: *Globe and Mail*, December 13, 1986.

Best Reaction to Realizing You're Going to Be the next Prime Minister of Canada: *So What Are the Boys Saying?: An Inside Look at Brian Mulroney in Power* by Michel Gratton (McGraw-Hill Ryerson, 1987).

ADDITIONAL SOURCES

Campbell, Avril P. *Sayings of Chairman Kim*. Robert Davies Publ., 1993.

Chichinskas, Pamela and Lynette, Stokes. *The Leaders Speak*. Penguin Books Canada, 1988

Colombo, John Robert. *New Canadian Quotations*. Hurtig, 1987.

————-.*Colombo's Concise Canadian Quotations*. Hurtig, 1974.

————-.*The Dictionary of Canadian Quotations*. Stoddart, 1991.

————-.*Colombo's All-Time Great Canadian Quotations*. Stoddart, 1994.

————-.*Metro's Goldwyn Mayor: The Complete Malapropisms of Allan Lamport*. Colombo and Company, 1995.

————-.*All About Us: A Collection of Occasional Humour*. Colombo and Company, 1998.

————-.*Famous Lasting Words: Great Canadian Quotations*. Douglas & McIntyre, 2000.

————-.*The Penguin Book of Canadian Jokes*. Penguin Books Canada, 2001.

————-.*The Penguin Book of More Canadian Jokes*. Penguin Books Canada, 2003.

Duhaime, Lloyd. *Hear! Hear! 125 Years of Debate in Canada's House of Commons*. Stoddart, 1992.

Katz, Eliakim. *Eh Canada?* Stoddart, 1999.

McIlroy, Thad. *Diefenbaker: Remembering the Chief*. Doubleday Canada, 1984.

Munro, John A. *The Wit and Wisdom of John Diefenbaker*. Hurtig, 1982.

Olive, David. *Political Babble: The 1,000 Dumbest Things Ever Said by Politicians*. John Wiley and Sons, 1992.

————.*Canadian Political Babble: A Cynic's Dictionary of Political Jargon.* John Wiley and Sons, 1993.

————.*More Political Babble: The Dumbest Things Politicians Ever Said.* John Wiley and Sons, 1996.

Schendlinger, Mary. *The Little Blonde Book of Kim Campbell.* Arsenal Pulp Press, 1993.

Wente, Margaret. *I Never Say Anything Provocative: Witticisms, Anecdotes and Reflections by Canada's Most Outspoken Politician.* P. Martin Associates, 1975.